First World War
and Army of Occupation
War Diary
France, Belgium and Germany

58 DIVISION
Divisional Troops
503 Field Company Royal Engineers
1 September 1915 - 22 February 1916

WO95/2996/1

The Naval & Military Press Ltd
www.nmarchive.com
Published in association with The National Archives

Published by

The Naval & Military Press Ltd

Unit 10 Ridgewood Industrial Park,

Uckfield, East Sussex,

TN22 5QE England

Tel: +44 (0) 1825 749494

www.naval-military-press.com

www.nmarchive.com

This diary has been reprinted in facsimile from the original. Any imperfections are inevitably reproduced and the quality may fall short of modern type and cartographic standards.

© **Crown Copyright**
Images reproduced by permission of The National Archives, London, England, 2015.

Contents

Document type	Place/Title	Date From	Date To
Heading	WO95/2996/1		
Heading	58th Division 503rd Field Coy R.E. 1915 Sep-1916 Feb And 1917 Jan-1919 May		
War Diary	Wickham Market	01/09/1915	30/09/1915
War Diary	Needham Market	02/10/1915	29/01/1916
War Diary	South Bourne B'Mouth to Needham Market	22/02/1916	22/02/1916

WO 95/2996/1

58TH DIVISION

503RD FIELD COY R.E.
~~JAN 1917 - MAY 1919.~~

1915 SEP — 1916 FEB
and
1917 JAN — 1919 MAY

Army Form C. 2118.

WAR DIARY
or
INTELLIGENCE SUMMARY

(Erase heading not required.)

Instructions regarding War Diaries and Intelligence Summaries are contained in F. S. Regs., Part II. and the Staff Manual respectively. Title pages will be prepared in manuscript.

Hour, Date, Place	Summary of Events and Information	Remarks and references to Appendices
1915 Sept 1 WICKHAM MARKET	Pontoon Rowing. Use of Spars. Miniature Range. Section Drill.	OMSJ
2 "	do	OMSJ
3 "	Musketry Instruction	OMSJ
4 "	do	OMSJ
5 "	Church Parade. 2/C MACPHAIL returns from NEWARK	OMSJ
6 "	2/LG JONES + MACPHAIL + 102 other ranks to GRAFHAM	OMSJ
7 "	for musketry course. Casting Bridging Spars from BUTLEY PRIORY	OMSJ
8 "	do	OMSJ
9 "	Turn out + Stand By 10 P.M. to 1 A.M. Routine. Turn out + Stand By 9.30 P.M. to 12.30 A.M.	OMSJ
10 "	Casting Bridging Superstructure (Technical) from Station	
11 "	Cookery Classes. 2/Lo JONES + MACPHAIL + detachment return from musketry course at GRAFHAM.	OMSJ
12 "	Section Drill. Rifle + Bayonet Exercise Church Parade	OMSJ
13 "	Section Drill. Voice Training J.D. Inspection of Horses by ADVS. Turn out + Stand By 8.30 P.M. to 1.40 A.M.	OMSJ

WAR DIARY or INTELLIGENCE SUMMARY

Army Form C. 2118.

(Erase heading not required.)

Instructions regarding War Diaries and Intelligence Summaries are contained in F.S. Regs., Part II. and the Staff Manual respectively. Title pages will be prepared in manuscript.

Hour, Date, Place	Summary of Events and Information	Remarks and references to Appendices
1915 Sept 14 WICKHAM MARKET	2Lt F.P.BRAY promoted Captain + Seconded for duty at ONGAR. S.M.E. 1E/29/7/15. Company Drill. Musketry. Visitation & Miniature Range. Pontoon Trestle Drill	
" 15	Section Drill. Pontoon Drill. Bayonet Exercises. Cash Fountain to ASHE ABBEY. Turn out & Stand By 8.20 P.M. to 1.40 A.M.	OMY OMY
" 16	Company Drill. Pontoon Drill. Indrometer & J.D. Sphia voltage & smoke guards for Bernd Pier Stores	OMY
" 17	Routine of work as 16 inst.	OMY
" 18	Pontoon Drill. Trestle Bridging. Indrometer & J.D.	OMY
" 19	Period of Vigilance ordered 6 P.M. Pack & prepare to move 2Lt J.S.JONES to SOUTHAMPTON to rejoin 1/1st Wessex Cry 2Lt E.L.MARTIN to BRIGHTLINGSEA for 6 weeks course Period of Vigilance ends 3.20 P.M.	OMY
" 20	Unpack vehicles. Pontoon Drill. Trestle Bridging. J.D. Sewing & Lindley " do	OMY OMY
" 21	" " do do	
" 22	Cpl. GUILFORD Bearer M. FISHER on promotion to 2 Lt. CSM. PAGE Drill. Trestle & Bridging. Repair to Ponny T. Lindley. 20 men to meet & bring 10 bs and from IPSWICH	OMY

Army Form C. 2118.

WAR DIARY
or
INTELLIGENCE SUMMARY

(Erase heading not required.)

Instructions regarding War Diaries and Intelligence Summaries are contained in F. S. Regs., Part II. and the Staff Manual respectively. Title pages will be prepared in manuscript.

Hour, Date, Place	Summary of Events and Information	Remarks and references to Appendices
1915		
Sept 23 WICKHAM MARKET	Infantry Drill. Burnt Pier Drill. Trestle, Muller Trestle Bridging	OMMJ
" 24 "	Cooking Test Cowls	OMMJ
" 25 "	do	OMMJ
" 26 "	Church Parade.	OMMJ
" 27 "	Burnt Pier Drill. Trestle Bridging. Pontoon Wheeling	OMMJ
" 28 "	do ; Pontoon Drill.	OMMJ
" 29 "	Bridging Specials. Cart Stores to Rail Station	OMMJ
" 30 "	Packing, Loading & Carting Stores & Baggage to Station	OMMJ

OMMStanton
Maj RE (TF)

O.C. 2/1st London Field Coy RE

WAR DIARY
or
INTELLIGENCE SUMMARY

(Erase heading not required.)

Instructions regarding War Diaries and Intelligence Summaries are contained in F. S. Regs., Part II. and the Staff Manual respectively. Title pages will be prepared in manuscript.

Hour, Date, Place	Summary of Events and Information	Remarks and references to Appendices
1915		
Oct 2 NEEDHAM MARKET	Move by route march to NEEDHAM MARKET — 4 officers 193 other ranks 58 horses + 12 vehicles.	ORW
" 3 "	2Lt R.S. MACPHAIL to SOUTHAMPTON to reinforce 1/1st London Field Coy overseas.	ORW
" 7 "	2Lts C.H. JOHNSON & J.T.F. HENDERSON from 3/1st London Field Coy report for duty.	ORW

MWJphinston
Major R.E. (T.F.)
O.C. 2/1st London Field Coy R.E.

Army Form C. 2118.

WAR DIARY
or
INTELLIGENCE SUMMARY   2/1st London Field Coy
(Erase heading not required.)

Hour, Date, Place	Summary of Events and Information	Remarks and references to Appendices
1915 Nov 4 NEEDHAM MARKET	Horses & mules placed in stables & shelters.	OMJ/F
" 6 "	2nd Lieut. D.E. CLERK reports for duty. 2nd Lieut E.L. MARTIN & L/Cpl HILL return from SME course at BRIGHTLINGSEA	OMJ/F
" 7 "	Lieut. C.H. JOHNSON. 2nd Corpl BALDERSTON & 1 Batman proceed to BRIGHTLINGSEA for 6 weeks SME Course.	OMJ/F
" 11 "	18 L.D. Horses received from AVONMOUTH.	OMJ/F
" 15 "	L/Cpl EDMONDS + Sappers DOWDESWELL, GRANT, BUNDOCK and BUSH transferred to Royal Flying Corps.	OMJ/F
" 17 "	Horse No. 11925 died. Twisted intestine.	OMJ/F
" " "	Horse No. 11907 died. Rupture of abdominal blood vessel.	OMJ/F
" 20 "	Sappers A.D. COOPER & A.E. READ proceed to WOOLWICH for course of "Repair of Service Bicycles". Sapper RADLEY to ST ALBANS for course at School of Cookery. Pte GRIMBOL (attached) returned to A.S.C.	OMJ/F
" 23 "	Armourer Sergt ROBINSON joins for temporary duty	OMJ/F
" 29 "	L/Corpl F.S. EDWARDS proceeds to ALDERSHOT for course of Physical Training + Bayonet fighting	OMJ/F

OMJ/Johnstone
Major RE (T.F.)
O.C. 2/1st London Field Coy RE(F)

WAR DIARY or INTELLIGENCE SUMMARY

Army Form C. 2118.

(Erase heading not required.)

Instructions regarding War Diaries and Intelligence Summaries are contained in F. S. Regs., Part II. and the Staff Manual respectively. Title pages will be prepared in manuscript.

Hour, Date, Place	Summary of Events and Information	Remarks and references to Appendices
NEEDHAM MARKET 2/12/15	No 1907 Sapr S.E. PURDAY died at 2/2nd Field Ambulance IPSWICH	Headquarters of 2nd London on Divisional Engineers 2/10th Bn. Corps.
4/12/15	Saprs A.B. COOPER and A.E. READ return from WOOLWICH	Course: Repair of Service Bicycles
10/12/15	Comp. Sergt ROBINSON leave on completion of duty	Repair of Arms
11/12/15	Sapr RADLEY returns from ST ALBANS	Cookery Class
13/12/15	Sapr KINGSTON proceeds to ST ALBANS	Cookery Class
14/12/15	Draft of recruits received from 3/1st London Field Coy	24 Sappers & 1 Driver
15/12/15	Orders received to hold unit in readiness to move to ALDERSHOT at short notice.	
19/12/15	Corpl F.J. BYWATER to be temp. Major & Lieut RANNAN late Temp. Captain	
20/12/15	No 1230 Sergt E.A. WAKE died at 2/2nd Field Ambulance IPSWICH from injuries accidentally sustained during demolitions at BAYLHAM.	
24/12/15	Funeral of Sergt E.A. WAKE at GREETING ST MARY.	
26/12/15	LCpl EDWARDS returns from ALDERSHOT Course	Physical Training Regmt Fighting
28/12/15	C.R.E. leaves for Staff Tour abroad.	(signed) REFF
31/12/15	2 Lieut DECLERK & 2nd Corpl MORRISON to BRIGHTLINGSEA S.M.E.	O.C. 2/1st London Field Coy R.E.(T.F)

Army Form C. 2118.

WAR DIARY
or
INTELLIGENCE SUMMARY

2/1st London Field Coy RE(TF)

(Erase heading not required.)

Instructions regarding War Diaries and Intelligence Summaries are contained in F. S. Regs., Part II. and the Staff Manual respectively. Title pages will be prepared in manuscript.

[Stamp: 58th LONDON DIVISION — 3 FEB 1916 — GENERAL STAFF]

Hour, Date, Place	Summary of Events and Information	Remarks and references to Appendices
NEEDHAM MARKET 1/2/16	Major F.P. BYWATER proceeds to CLAYDON to assume command of 1/5th London Field Coy RE (TF)	OMM
" 3/2/16	Lieut C.H. JOHNSON transferred to Royal Flying Corps & proceeds to READING	OMM
" 11/2/16	2nd Lieut H.A. SCOTT transferred from 3/1st London Field Coy RE(TF) to join for duty.	OMM
" 15/2/16	Orders received to prepare units for overseas.	OMM
" 22/2/16	2nd Lieuts E.L. MARTIN and J.T.F. HENDERSON to be Lieuts 22/2/16	OMM
" 24/2/16	18 other ranks posted to FELIXSTOWE (Musketry Course)	OMM
" 29/2/16	2nd Lieut J.A. MERCER transferred from 3/1st London Field Coy RE(TF) OMM (L.D.O. 25.7.2/2/11/16)	OMM

O.W.I. Johnstone
Maj RE(TF)
O.C. 2/1st London Field Coy RE(TF)

WAR DIARY
or
INTELLIGENCE SUMMARY.

2/1st Wessex Field Coy. R.E.

Army Form C. 2118.

(Erase heading not required.)

Hour, Date, Place	Summary of Events and Information	Remarks and references to Appendices
SOUTHBOURNE B'MOUTH to NEEDHAM MARKET 22-2-16	The Company moved from SOUTHBOURNE to NEEDHAM MARKET by rail, leaving CHRISTCHURCH Station at 1.50 P.M. 22-2-16 and arriving at NEEDHAM MARKET at 11.50 P.M. 22-2-16. Moved into Billets vacated by 2/1st London Field Coy. R.E.	O/S O/S C. Trumper Major Commanding 2/1st Wessex Field Coy R.E. 3-3-16